If You Wake a SKUNK

Written by
CAROL DOERINGER

Illustrated by
FLORENCE WEISER

SHHH...

Tiptoe by. Don't make a peep.
It's daytime, so the skunk's asleep.
If he's disturbed, he might just spray.

Let him snooze...

Now sneak away.

You inched ahead and took a peek.
But if he sprays you . . . you will REEK.

For weeks, you'll stink from head to toe.
If you're smart, you'll turn and go.

OOPS!

You sneezed. The skunk has stirred,
   and he's not sure what he just heard.

Beware . . .
   He will investigate.

So, ease on out.

   Right now.

   Don't wait.

Silly you, still standing there.
See his nostrils?
Watch them flare.

Sniff...He gets
a whiff of you.

Shoo! Before he *sees* you, too.

NOOO...

He turns...

He sees your face,

Hit the road.

Make tracks.

Now, race!

Don't you see that steady stare?
You've been warned.
Get out of there!

I can't believe you missed that cue . . .

NOW, EEK!
He's running right at you!

He stops! His front paws stamp the ground . . .

A handstand!
You must turn around.

Now he waves
his twitchy tail.

Get the message. You should bail!

See him snarling?

Hear that hiss?

If he sprays, he will not miss.

That stinky stuff will stick like glue.

Do you want his stench on you?

You're out of time.

YOU MUST RETREAT!

At last! You changed your mind. You fled!

But wait . . .
    Could you have been misled?

When skunks use up the stink they store,
it takes a while to make some more.

When they're empty, you can't tell.
And as for this one, well . . .

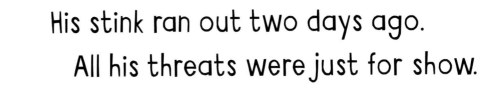

His stink ran out two days ago.
All his threats were just for show.

SKUNKS AND THEIR STINK DEFENSE

Skunks are gentle creatures that will avoid conflict if they can. Usually, they spray only when they believe they're in danger—as a last resort. The musk smells like rotten eggs.

What happens if you startle a skunk? The skunk will be scared . . . of YOU! It will stare and may hiss at you, arch its back, and raise its tail. It will stomp its front feet. Spotted skunks, like the one in this book, perform most of these moves while doing a handstand. These are all warnings: The skunk is telling you to leave.

If you ignore its warning signals, the skunk may spray. It will curve its body so both its nose and rear end point at you. If it sprays, the skunk will aim at your eyes. A stream of stink will fly up to fifteen feet!

A skunk can usually spray five times before using up its musk. If it empties its scent gland, the skunk will need up to ten days to recharge. But you can't know if a skunk's gland is empty. So, if you ever encounter a skunk, walk away—don't wait for a warning!

SKUNK FACTS

The most common skunk in North America is the striped skunk. You might also encounter the hooded skunk, the hog-nosed skunk, or the spotted skunk.

Skunks are usually about as big as house cats. The spotted skunk is smaller, about the size of a large tree squirrel.

Skunks are nocturnal—they sleep during the day. At night, they forage. They are omnivores, meaning they eat all kinds of food, including insects, fruits, small rodents, and bird eggs. They also eat garbage and pet food when they can find it!

Skunks prefer to live in fields or woods. They dig burrows or take over a fox or a woodchuck's old burrow. In summer, they often sleep above ground in brush piles or hollow logs. If they find themselves in cities or suburbs, they might make their homes under decks and porches.

LEARN MORE

Pringle, Laurence, and Garchinsky, Kate, illustrator. *The Secret Life of the Skunk*. Honesdale, PA: Boyds Mill Press, 2019.

Mason, Adrienne and Ogle, Nancy Gray, illustrator. *Skunks*. Tonawanda, NY: Kids Can Press, 2006.

Schuh, Mari. *Skunks*. North Mankato, MN: Capstone Press, 2017.

TO ELLIE, VINCE, MAEVE, AND DANNY. WHETHER SPIDERS, SKUNKS, OR SOMETHING ELSE THAT SEEMS SCARY, MAY YOU ALWAYS PAUSE TO SEE THE WONDER IN WILDLIFE.

–NANA

Text Copyright © 2023 Carol Doeringer
Illustration Copyright © 2023 Florence Weiser
Design Copyright © 2023 Sleeping Bear Press

SLEEPING BEAR PRESS™

2395 South Huron Parkway, Suite 200
Ann Arbor, MI 48104
www.sleepingbearpress.com

Printed and bound in China.

10 9 8 7 6 5 4 3 2 1

Library of Congress Cataloging-in-Publication Data

Names: Doeringer, Carol, author. | Weiser, Florence, illustrator.
Title: If you wake a skunk / written by Carol Doeringer ;
illustrated by Florence Weiser.
Description: Ann Arbor, MI : Sleeping Bear Press, [2023] | Audience: Grades 2-3.
| Summary: When a pair of campers stumble upon a skunk, they
repeatedly dismiss its defensive warning signs. Includes fun facts about skunks.
Identifiers: LCCN 2022038519 | ISBN 9781534111721 (hardcover) Subjects: CYAC:
Stories in rhyme. | Skunks—Fiction. | Animal defenses—Fiction. |
LCGFT: Stories in rhyme. | Picture books.
Classification: LCC PZ8.3.D673 If 2023 | DDC [E]—dc23
LC record available at https://lccn.loc.gov/2022038519